The Life Cycle of an

D1717109

Trevor Terry &
Margaret Linton

Illustrated by
Jackie Harland

The Bookwright Press
New York · 1988

First published in the
United States in 1988 by
The Bookwright Press
387 Park Avenue South
New York, NY 10016

First published in 1987 by
Wayland (Publishers) Limited
61 Western Road, Hove
East Sussex, BN3 1JD, England

ISBN 0-531-18162-6

Library of Congress Catalog Card Number: 87-71473

Typeset in the UK by DP Press Limited, Sevenoaks, Kent
Printed by Casterman S.A., Belgium

Contents

All the words that are
in **bold** are explained in
the glossary on page 31.

Where do ants live?

Ants are busy little **insects**. They live in nests. Different kinds of ants build in different kinds of places. Some ants make small hills in meadows or woods. Others build under stones and paving slabs.

Ants live together

Ants live and work together just like we do. A **queen ant, male ants** and **worker ants** all live in one nest. The queen is the biggest. She lays the eggs. The worker ants are tiny. They do all the work. There may be thousands of ants in one nest.

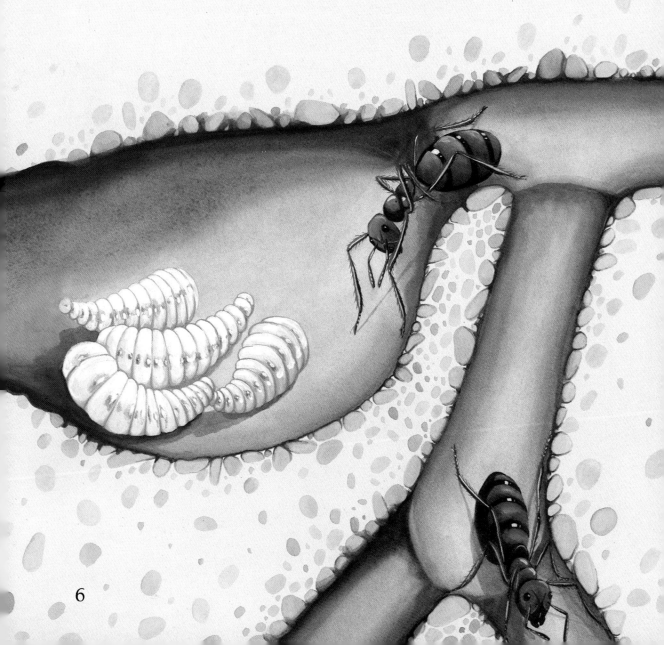

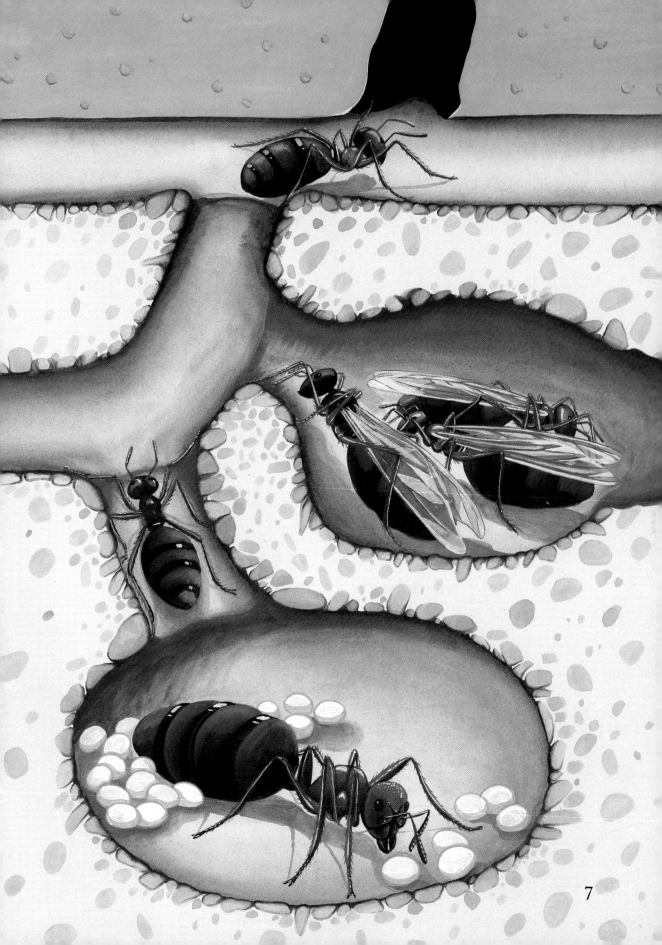

8

Young queens and males

On a warm day in summer, young queens and male ants fly up into the sky to **mate**. This is called the **marriage flight**. After the marriage flight, the male ants die. Now the young queen ants get ready to lay their first eggs.

The queen starts a nest

First of all, young queen ants look for good places to build their nests. They will stay there for the rest of their lives. When a queen has found the right place, she breaks off her wings. Then she begins to dig. She makes a small tunnel under the ground.

The queen lays her eggs

When the tunnel is ready, the queen lays her first eggs. As the weather gets colder, the queen goes to sleep. She stays asleep all winter. She wakes up in the spring and begins to look after her eggs. She licks them to keep them clean.

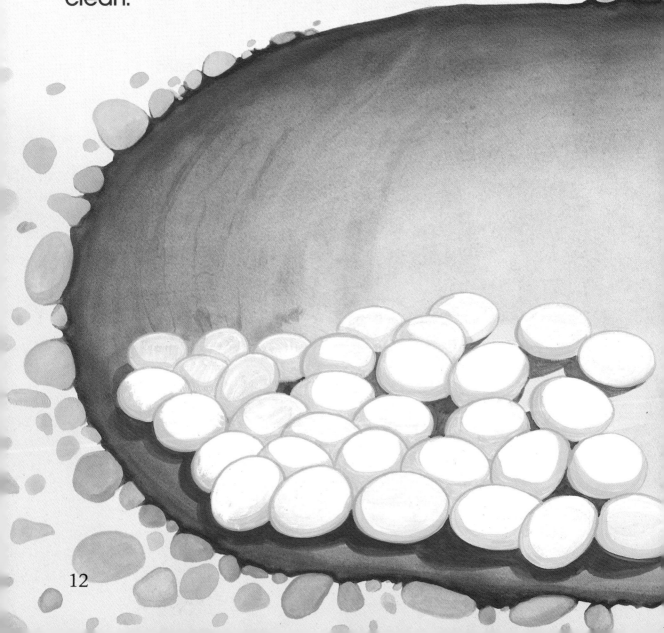

The eggs hatch

After a few weeks the eggs hatch into white **grubs** called **larvae**. Each **larva** has a soft body, a mouth and tiny sharp jaws. The queen feeds them. The larvae grow very quickly. They grow too big for their skins. The old skins drop off and new skins grow. This is called **molting**.

Worker ants are born

Soon the larvae are fully grown. Each larva makes a case around itself, called a **cocoon**. The larva inside the cocoon becomes a **pupa**. After a while the pupa changes into a young worker ant. The queen helps the young ants to come out of their cocoons.

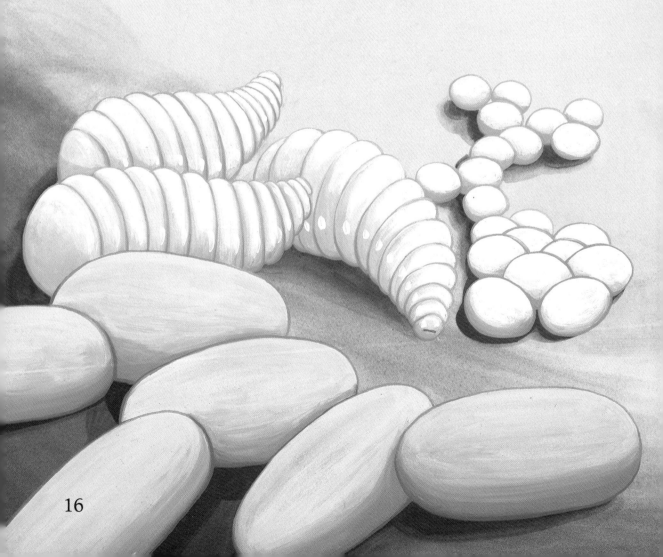

16

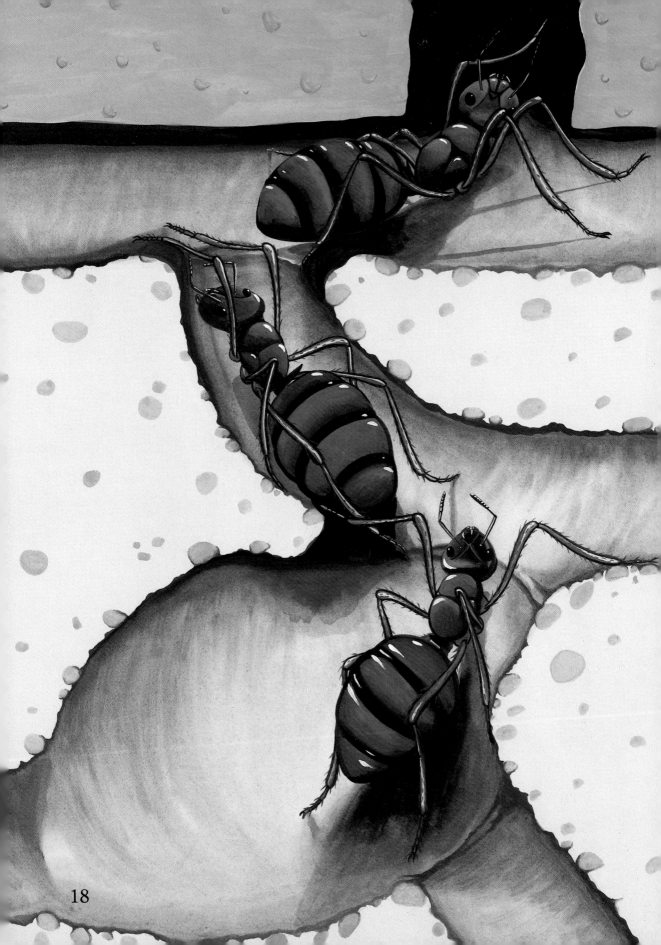

Working ants

The new ants have soft, pale skins. Soon they begin to change. Their color turns darker. Their skins get harder. They begin to do all kinds of jobs. Some go out to look for food. Ants like drops of sweet juice called honeydew. Honeydew is made by insects called **aphids**.

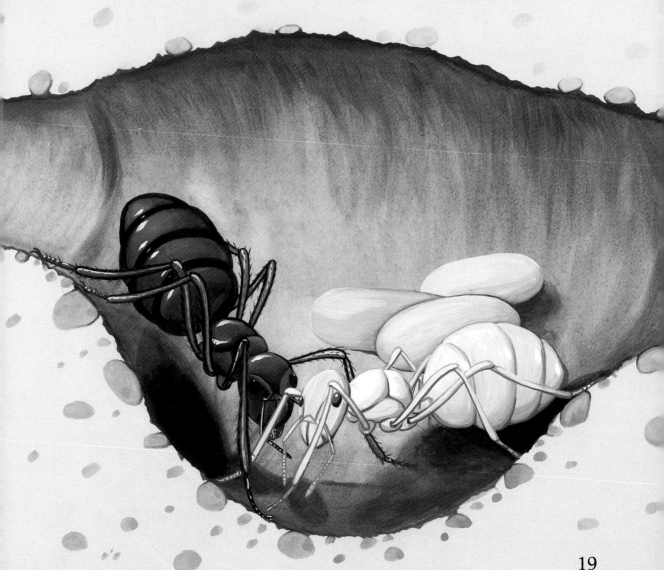

The worker ants and the queen

Some worker ants begin to look after the queen. They feed her by putting food from their own mouths into her mouth. They lick her to keep her clean. All this time the queen has been laying more and more eggs. There are more and more larvae and cocoons in the nest.

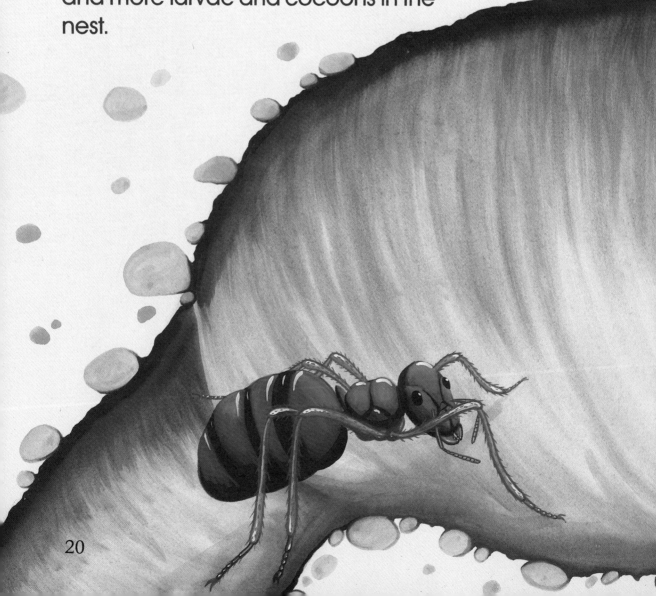

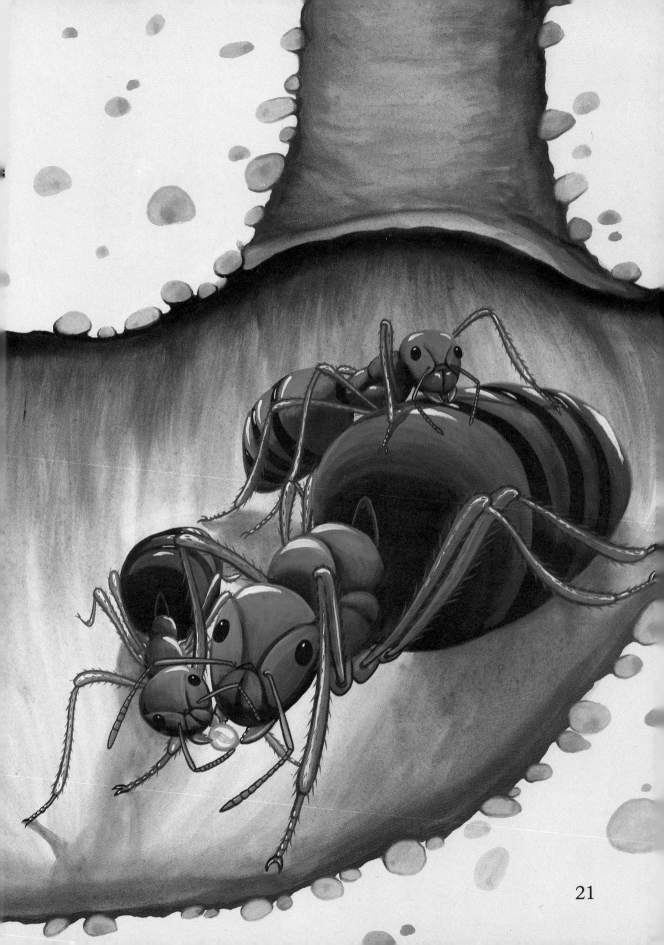

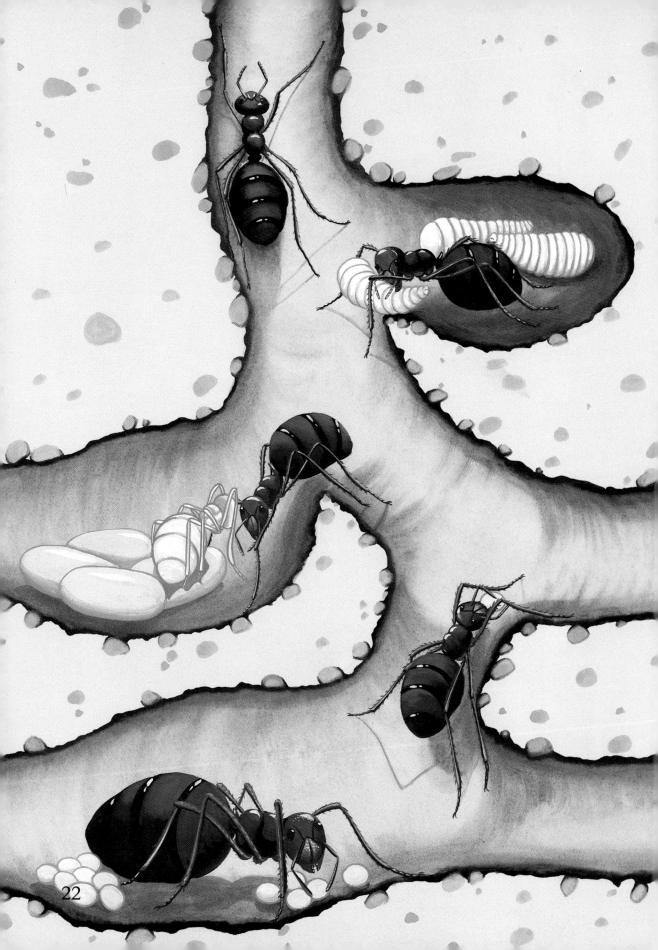

The nest in the summer

The ants build more tunnels in the summer. They keep the nest clean and tidy. Some worker ants leave the nest to look for food. Others feed the larvae and young ants. **Nurse ants** move the eggs, larvae and cocoons to different parts of the nest.

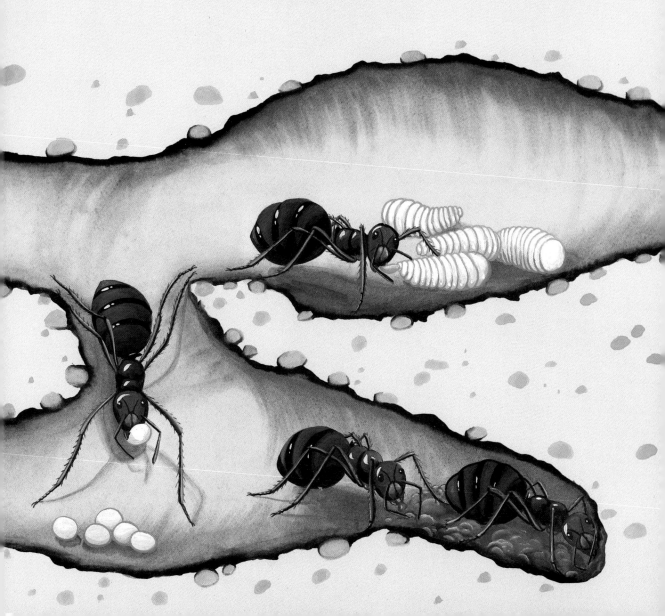

New queens and males

During the summer the queen lays some different eggs. These eggs will turn into male ants and young queen ants. The larvae are bigger. The workers feed them on special food. The male ants and young queen ants have wings. They are bigger than the worker ants.

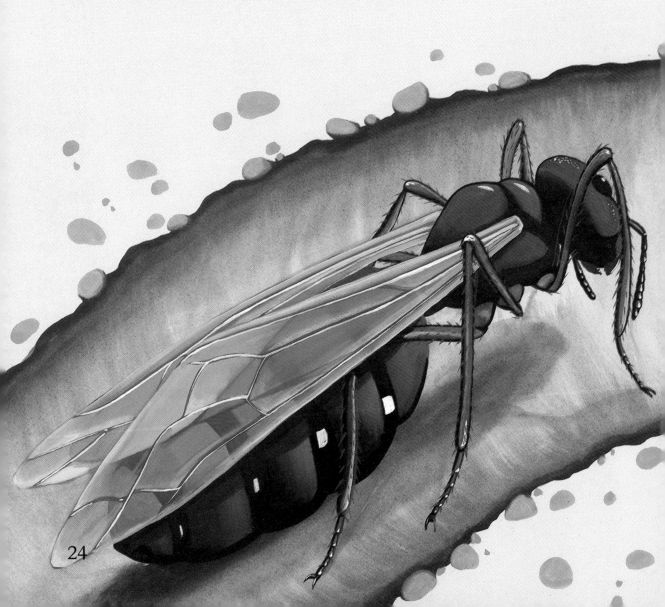

24

The queens and males fly off

On a warm day in summer, the males and young queens come out of the nest. Worker ants come out too, and they all scurry around. Then the males and young queens fly up into the sky for the marriage flight. Now the story begins all over again.

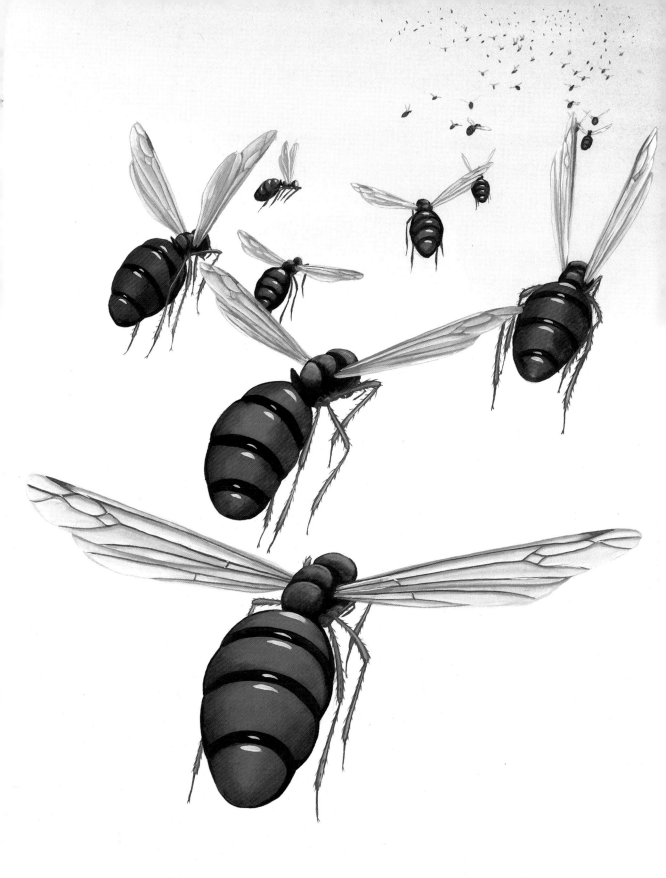

Keeping ants

You can make an ants' nest like the one
in the picture. Put some moist soil in a
large jam jar. Stand the jar in a dish of
water to keep the ants from getting out.
Look under big stones and find some
garden ants. Ask an adult to help you.
Put the ants in the jar. Cover it with a
piece of plywood or hardboard that
has a hole in the middle.

Spread a little honey on a small piece
of bark. Put this on top of the cover. Ants
will eat cake crumbs, too. Ants do not
like light, so cover the dish and the jar
with a cardboard box. After a few days,
take the box off. See if the ants have
started to make their tunnels.
Remember to put the box back again.

The life cycle of an ant

How many stages of the life cycle can you remember? Here is the life cycle of a queen ant.

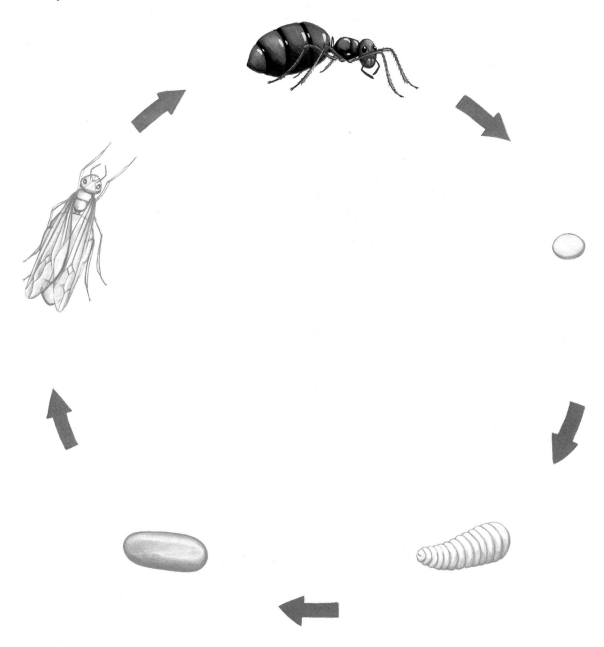

Glossary

Aphids Small insects that suck juices from plants for food.

Cocoon The case that surrounds a pupa.

Grub The larva of an insect, such as a beetle.

Insects Small animals without backbones. They have three pairs of legs, and usually two pairs of wings. Their bodies are covered with a hard skin.

Larvae Grubs that hatch from an egg. One grub is called a **larva**. Lots of grubs are called **larvae**.

Male ants Ants that mate with young queens during the marriage flight.

Marriage flight The time when young queens and male ants leave the nest and fly away to mate.

Mate To join as a male (father) and female (mother) in order to have babies.

Molting Shedding skin or feathers. When the caterpillar (or larva) gets too big for its skin, the old skin comes off and a new skin grows.

Nurse ants Ants who help the queen ant to look after her eggs. They also move the larvae and cocoons around the nest.

Pupa A resting stage when a larva changes into an adult insect.

Queen ant The female ant, which lays eggs.

Worker ants Small female ants without wings. They do all the different jobs in the nest.

Finding out more

Here are some books to read to find out more.

Animal Homes by Malcolm Penny. Franklin Watts (The Bookwrigh Press), 1987.
Ants by Cynthia Overbeck. Lerner Publications, 1982.
Insects Do the Strangest Things by Leonora and Arthur Hornblow Random House, 1968.
Look at Insects revised edition, by Rena K. Kirkpatrick. Raintree Publishers, 1985.
Small World of Ants by David Cook. Franklin Watts, 1981.

Index